THIS
BOOK
BELONGS TO

_____

Warner Books, Inc., 666 Fifth Avenue, New York, NY 10103
Ⓦ A Warner Communications Company

Printed in the United States of America
First Warner Juvenile Books Printing: March 1988
10 9 8 7 6 5 4 3 2 1

Library of Congress Cataloging-in-Publication Data

Gilchrist, Guy.
    Counting tiny dinos.

    Summary: In this rhyming story, playful dinosaurs
introduce numbers from one to ten.
    [1. Counting.   2. Dinosaurs—Fiction.   3. Stories
in rhyme]   I. Title.
PZ8.3.G39Co   1988   [E]   87-40333
ISBN 1-55782-011-2

THIS BOOK IS FOR HAPPY-GO-LUCKY TOM BRENNER

Guy Gilchrist's
COUNTING
TINY
DINOS

A BOOK OF NUMBERS

WARNER
JUVENILE
BOOKS

A Warner Communications Company

NEW YORK

1 Tiny Dino
Above the trees she flew.

She finds another Tiny Dino!
Now there are 2

2 Tiny Dinos playing by the sea.
1 ran out of the water!
Now there are **3**

3 Tiny Dinos playing by the shore.

1 jumped down from a palm tree!
Now there are **4**

4 Tiny Dinos
splash, swim and dive.

Another Dino comes to play!
Now there are 5

5 Tiny Dinos playing sneaky Dino tricks.

"Boo" say the Dinos!
Now there are 6

6 Tiny Dinos
look up toward the heavens.

Counting flying birdosaurs!
They count 7

8! 8! They ate 8

8 big sandwiches
sure taste great!

Tiny Dinos count **9** stars
in a nighttime sky.

Now there are **10** as
a shooting star flies by!

Tired Tiny Dinos counting sheep.

1, 2, 3, 4, 5…*snore!*
Oops! They've gone to sleep!